Ossian Herbert Lang

Basedow : his educational work and principles

Ossian Herbert Lang

Basedow : his educational work and principles

ISBN/EAN: 9783337215255

Printed in Europe, USA, Canada, Australia, Japan

Cover: Foto ©Andreas Hilbeck / pixelio.de

More available books at **www.hansebooks.com**

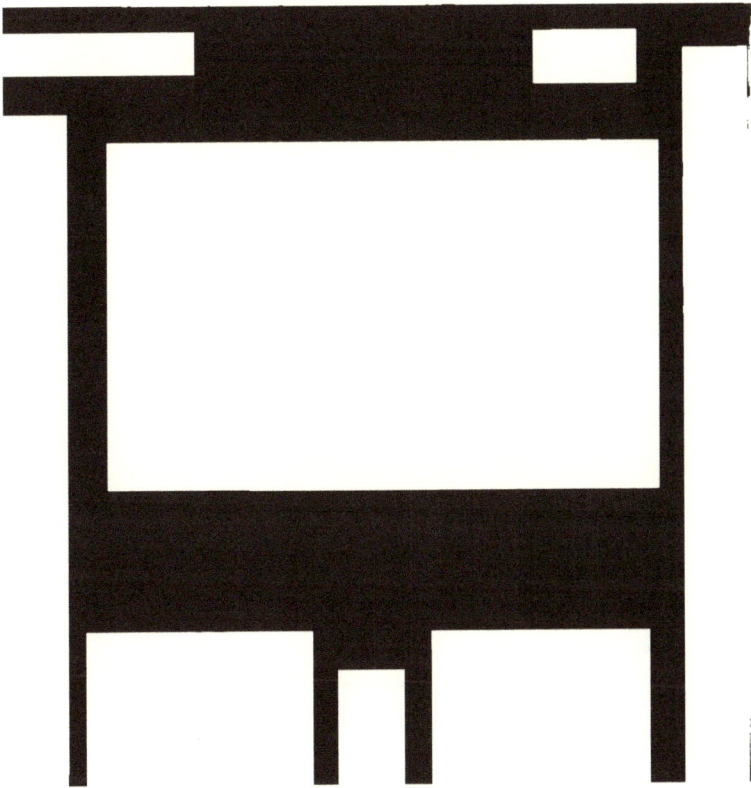

PREFACE.

In giving a sketch of Basedow's life and work, the writer has confined himself to what appeared to him the most valuable and characteristic ideas of the great school-reformer. The main object of this monograph is to interest the teachers in the study of the Basedovian system of education.

It cannot be said that Basedow discovered new foundation principles of education. He based his educational system on those principles of Comenius, Locke, and other great thinkers before him, which his own experience and the careful observation and investigation of the nature of the child and of the studies had found to be fundamental truths. Through the rational and persistent application of these principles, he succeeded in bringing about a complete change in the whole state of education and instruction.

The effects of this famous revolution can be traced through the whole era of progress that the science of education has made since his time.

FOUNDATION PRINCIPLES OF BASEDOW'S SYSTEM :
Everything according to the laws of Nature, p. 10. / 2

THE FORMATION OF CHARACTER OF MORE VALUE THAN THE ACQUISITION OF KNOWLEDGE, pp. 19, 27. 2 /

4 *Preface.*

SENSE-PERCEPTION THE BASIS OF ALL KNOWING,
p. 8.

Basedow's ideas on *physical and manual training* (pp.
4, 21, 24), on *state supervision of education* (p. 20), on the
training of teachers (p. 12), on the *qualifications of the
teacher* (p. 20), and on *aiming at the happiness of pupils*
(pp. 4, 16, 17, 23), will be found very suggestive.

O. H. L.

BASEDOW.

Basedow's Youth.—John Bernard Basedow was born in Hamburg on September 12, 1723. His father, a wig-maker, was rude and severe, and his mother is described as nervous and melancholy almost to madness. His boyhood, as may be expected, was by no means a happy one. He had been destined to follow the profession of his father, but ran away from home when about fourteen years old, became the servant of a country physician in Holstein, and did not return till his father promised to send him to college. In 1741 Basedow entered the Hamburg Johanneum, a renowned classic high-school. His teachers, preceiving his extraordinary gifts, predicted that he would some day become "one of the greatest thinkers and promoters of the common weal." In 1744 Basedow was sent to the University of Leipzig to study theology. He was negligent in the attendance of the regular lectures, studying mainly in private. He was particularly interested in Wolf's "Philosophy of Reason." This work influenced him greatly, placing him, as he explained, "in a centre between Christianism and naturalism."

5

Wants to Become a Reformer.—Rathmann, an impartial biographer and careful observer, informs us that Basedow "loved liberty in thought and action above everything else. Revolt against every restraint, against every limitation, had become his second nature, because he had to fight so much against it from his youth up." He felt himself called upon to become a reformer of mankind. Besides Wolf's Philosophy, which probably played an important part in turning his thoughts to reform, he read, while at Leipzig, also the writings of Plutarch, Quintilian, Locke, Rollin, and other educationists.

A Private Tutor at Borghorst.—From 1749 to 1753 he was the tutor of a little boy of the Danish privy-councillor Von Quaalen, at Borghorst. His mind was filled with ideas of reform, and carrying them out in the education of his pupil he laid the foundation of his educational work. Contrary to prevalent views, he believed that happiness of the children be a legitimate aim in education. He held the freest intercourse with his little pupil, engaged in all his childish games, and thus gained and cherished his love and confidence, and found an opportunity of studying the child's thoughts and inclinations. Conversation and play were his invitations to knowledge. He laid much stress upon physical development. Early rising, marching, swimming, riding, dancing, etc., were included in the order of the day. Owing to his original manner of teaching, Basedow attained the best results. In teaching Latin, for instance, he began by pointing to objects and giving their Latin names.

His pupil, in a very short time, learned to speak Latin almost as well as his native language. Basedow himself learned French after the same manner, of the governess of the house.

First Educational Writings.—The news of Basedow's enviable success at Borghorst, and particularly his manner of teaching, had spread and created quite a sensation in pedagogic circles. This encouraged him to summarize theoretically what and how he had taught his pupil, in a Latin dissertation, "On the best and hitherto unknown Method of Teaching the Children of Noblemen." This treatise he presented to the University of Kiel in 1752, and obtained the degree of Master of Arts. He attacked in this pamphlet the faulty, unnatural methods of the schools of his time, and proposed a shorter and more pleasant way, which he called "the natural way of teaching children." In the same year he published an "Account of how said Method was actually put in Practice, and what it has Effected."

Professor at Soroe.—In 1753 Basedow obtained a position as Professor of Morality and Polite Literature in the Danish Academy of Young Noblemen of Soroe (Zealand). His professional lectures stirred up a sensation. His personal intensity, the wit and happy notions that sparkled through his discourse, and above all his cheerful and enthusiastic eloquence, drew a large attendance to his lecture-room. From all parts of Denmark the young noblemen came, with their instructors, to hear the young professor, who was so different from the mummyvisaged academic monologists of the time. The be-wigged and bepowdered colleagues hated "Mad Base-dow," as they called him, particularly, because he, a foreigner, a German, was made the object of so much admiration in their own native country.

Marries.—Basedow had married the French governess of the house Von Quaalen before he came to Soroe. Over his studies and professional work he utterly neg-lected her, and the poor woman died after a few months of unhappiness. In 1755 he married the daughter of a Danish clergyman, a very intelligent and amiable woman. Basedow never fully appreciated the treasure he had won in her. He was, as he used to say, "not made for matrimonial life, as he had married the public."

Called Unorthodox.—As Basedow's popularity as a teacher increased, he was called upon to lecture also on theology. This gave his envious colleagues a chance to expose him to ceaseless annoyances. He was too upright to hide those opinions which could be turned against him. He fearlessly pointed out to his students all doc-trines and ceremonies of the established church which were without spiritual warrant. The more the religious sharpers of the faculty denounced him on that account, the more his spirit of contradiction grew. In 1758 he published his "Practical Philosophy," and came out boldly with his religious views. His opponents imme-diately drew up a formal accusation and presented it to the king. Basedow's friends at Copenhagen interceded in his behalf, among them the Bishop of Zealand, the

renowned J. A. Cramer, and the famous Danish states-
man Count Von Bernstorff. The government acquitted
Basedow, but removed him to the academic school at
Altona.

Aims at Educational Reform.—Basedow had begun to
feel that little was to be done against the old system
by attempting to set its slaves aright. He hoped and
firmly believed that the promotion of human happiness
could be effected only by a better education of youth.
He therefore had improved every occasion by designing
plans and preparing for the laying of the corner-stone
of a new and better education. The " Practical Philosophy " contained two chapters—" On Education" and
" On the Instruction of Children." These formed the
basis on which Basedow built up his system of education. In this work he already indicated that the progress of the time had made a complete reform necessary,
and that he had often thought of inaugurating the
change. He also gives an outline of his method of
teaching through conversation and play, and many valuable hints on the physical training of children.

The Educational Campaign Opens.—Basedow came to
Altona in 1760. His life in this city presents a most
tumultuous scene. Hitherto the public had not heeded
his propositions in regard to a change in the state of
education. He now went on the war-path against igno-
rance, superstition, and apathy in educational matters.
He intended to impress on the people the dangers of
the old conventionalism, to create a general desire for
reform, and to call their attention to his plans. His

tumultuous proceedings were the signal for the revival
of educational activity. In the struggle against the bas-
tille of uncompromising dogmatism, which domineered
in the shattered and benighted country, "Basedow bore
the dangers alone, and therefore is worthy of a seat of
honor among the leaders, who fought for the spiritual
freedom of the eighteenth century" (Max Mueller).

Writes Books.—In 1764 Basedow published the
"Philalethy." This was almost immediately followed
by three other volumes, which appeared under the title
"Methodical Instruction of the Youth in both Natural
and Biblical Religion." Then appeared "First Elements
of Religion," and in 1765 "Theoretical System of
Sound Reason." His plan of a school reform was clearly
outlined in these words. In teaching, he insisted on
sense-impressions, on "placing before the children objects or drawings of them." He spoke of the necessity
of a good text-book, which would contain all that a child
should learn, and would give at the same time a rational
plan of instruction. In the "Methodical Instruction"
he announced his intention of carrying out the reform
of the schools. He added that "human society can be
made better only through a complete amelioration of
the schools. However, nothing will be accomplished by
reasoning about the mistakes and disorder of instruction, as long as there are no means of bettering them."
He then explained that the first and most necessary
means would be good school-books. He also demanded
reform in the treatment of philosophic science in the
universities.

Is Attacked.—These heterodox writings raised a storm of opposition in the clerical camp. They were declared "antichristians, wicked, and heathenish." Some literary yelpers demanded a public apology of the author. Basedow at once published his "Extorted Polemic Discussions," "Attempt at Liberal Dogmatics," "Trials of Time," etc. Books and pamphlets followed in almost incredibly quick succession. Basedow could not be nonplussed by literary attacks. "He was extensively read, and had skill in the fencing tricks of disputation."

Coercive Measures Applied.—Orthodoxy resorted to coercive measures. Basedow and his family were excommunicated by the Lutheran clergy of Hamburg and Altona. The Legislature of Hamburg condemned his writings as heretical, and ordered them to be burnt. Teachers who used his books were threatened with banishment. Other German cities followed the example of Hamburg.

Writes the "Appeal."—Basedow was prepared for a crisis. He had aroused the people from their long slumber. The time for a realization of his plans, for the change of education, had come. In 1768 he sent out his "Appeal to Philanthropists and Men of Wealth on Schools and Studies and their Influence on the Common Weal." This manifesto was the signal for a general revolt against the hebetation methods, memory-cramming, and other atrocities of educational fogeyism. Its influence can be traced through a great part of the epoch of activity in the interests of schools, which succeeded the "Appeal."

It was the first important and most valuable educational tractate of the eighteenth century; and, as a great educationist has said, "no other treatise has created so widespread and practical an educational interest since Luther's 'Address to the Councillors.'"

Outlines an Educational Reform.—In the "Appeal" Basedow explained the foundation principle of his educational system, "*Everything according to nature*," and submitted his plan. Firstly, a great illustrated work, the "Elementary," was to be published, from which the children were to be instructed. Then a model school should be established, where teachers would be prepared in the theory and practice of the new education. With these teachers a school might be started next. Thus they would get better school-books, better teachers, and better schools. He then went on : "In ten or twelve years the fruit of this change will have ripened. We will have better-instructed professors in the universities and better-educated men of letters; and as the dignity of our national character chiefly depends on these men, it will also be better."

How His Plans were Received.—Basedow had set about the work of realizing his scheme. The "Elementary" was to be completed first. He succeeded in convincing the people that a better education meant a better and happier future for themselves and for the coming generations. He won them completely to his purpose. His plan of an "Elementary" rose more and more in their favor. He received so many letters, contributions, and inquiries of enthusiastic friends, that it became necessary for him to publish several papers in response. In 1768 and 1769 he issued "Conversations with Philanthropists;" in 1769, "Aim, Possibility, and Proof of the Elementary;" from 1770 to 1771 "Quarterly News of the Elementary." The productive author was bound to keep alive the general interest he had kindled. Every one of these writings brought explanations and illustrations of the proposed reform measures. He kept on attacking the routine work of the schools, and often took the literary sledge-hammers to quiet his opponents.

Writes the "Book of Method."—The first part of the "Elementary," the "Book of Method," appeared in 1770. This famous manual was undoubtedly the greatest of Basedow's educational writings. In ultra-traditional plans and principles the author exhibited his system of physical, moral, and intellectual education. The author not only exposed the actual state of school instruction with all its glaring defects, but he also urged the people to the speedy realization of thorough reform measures. He enforced the specific duties and responsibilities of educators. He demanded the emancipation of the schools from the control of the church, emphatically declaring that the state have a right to look to the education of every one of its subjects, and should therefore also assume the duty of supervising it. In short, the "Book of Method" was full of valuable suggestions. It set the educators to thinking, and has been a powerful motor in bringing about a change in school instruction.

Plans a Teachers' Seminary.—In less than four years
three new editions of the "Book of Methods" were
called for. One of these editions contained a "Plan of
a new Seminary for Children, Teachers, and Servants."
The author desired that a model school should be established, where the plans and principles laid down in the
"Book of Method" would be exemplified. This plan
soon found equal favor with the author's previous writings. It marked another progress in the history of
education: the time of teachers' seminaries began. The
Duke of Dessau called Basedow to his capital, there to
exemplify the scheme, as soon as the "Elementary"
would be completed.

Publishes the "Elementary."—In Dessau, Basedow
completed his "Elementary." It appeared in 1774, in
four volumes. Its success was truly astonishing. Not
only was a second edition called for, but it was translated
also into French, English, Russian, and other languages.
To-day the work is best known as the "Orbis Pictus of
the Eighteenth Century;" but Goethe, who in his youth
had been taught from the similar work of Comenius,
thought that "it is without those palpable methodical
advantages which we must acknowledge in the works of
Comenius." The "Elementary" has certainly never
been what its author and his enthusiastic admirers
claimed for it. Nevertheless it was a great work, because it left considerable traces behind. It started the
so-called "popular literature," and brought the readers,
as we now have them, into the school-room.

Plans to Establish a Model Institute.—Soon after the appearance of the " Elementary," Basedow went to work to realize the second part of his reform, namely, the establishment of a model institute " for the preparation of teachers in the theory and practice of the new education." He intended to name it " Philanthropin," the school of true humanity. Its name was to give evidence of its object—the education of youth in accordance with the laws of nature and humanity. In the projected school Basedow intended to exemplify his whole scheme of education, and to promote the dissemination of his principles. He intended to get the best of teachers. All instruction was to be founded on sense-impressions. Gymnastics, manual training, and other technical branches were to be introduced. He insisted upon getting "the best of models, the most perfect machines, and a library of useful books. The Philanthropin was to be a model in every direction. This required a considerable outlay. The Duke of Dessau granted an extensive building, surrounded by beautiful gardens. Basedow himself gave 3000 dollars and tried to raise the rest " by winning the people's hearts and purses" for this purpose.

The Philanthropin is Opened.—On December 27, 1774, the famous Philanthropin was opened with great festivities. Basedow and his friends entertained the best of hopes for a grand and glorious future. The great philosopher Kant, who firmly believed that a revolution in school education could be brought about best by " a school, which would be modelled after the true and genuine method and conducted by enlightened men with noble-minded zeal," warmly commended Basedow's institution to the public. Father Oberlin, the well-known German philanthropist, spoke enthusiastically of the Philanthropin, and was ever ready to solicit contributions for its support. Other great men who indorsed Basedow's work, such as the two philosophical writers Mendlessohn and Iselin, and the renowned Lavater.

Meets with Difficulties.—The Philanthropin was the first non-sectarian, a purely secular school. There was a stumbling-block for public opinion, which clung to the traditional church-school. Parents were continually warned from the pulpits not to send their children to that "God-forsaken Philanthropin." Rusty "scholemasters" ridiculed "that play-school at Dessau." In short, there were forces enough at work to keep up the prejudice of the masses. The result was that many parents withheld their children from the institution.

Publishes "Pedagogic Record."—Basedow noticed that his adversaries were only too successful in stirring the public feeling to the disadvantage of his institution. Immediately he set about to convince the people of the excellencies of the school. Accordingly he issued an educational journal, "The Pedagogic Record." The primary purpose of this publication was to furnish the friends of the Institution with reports of the work being done, and to counteract the misrepresentations of his gainsayers. The first number appeared in 1776, and contained an invitation to a great public examination, which was to be held at the Philanthropin in May of the same year.

The Examination.—When the examination of the Philanthropin was held there were many prominent men present, who had come from far and near to see and hear for themselves what Basedow had accomplished. They found only a small number of pupils, but, according to the reports of impartial witnesses, the result was surprisingly favorable. One of the visitors published a detailed account of the examination, under the title "Fred's Journey to Dessau." The number of pupils increased, and many new and influential educators came into Basedow's camp.

His Defects and Overwork.—One thing must be admitted here—Basedow was not fit to be at the head of the Philanthropin. He was too capricious and too easily excited for a prudent performance of his duties. Unfortunately he was lacking in self-command and perseverance. He felt this himself and confessed it publicly, and, shortly after the examination, turned the management over to Campe. For a short time everything looked favorable again, but Basedow began to mistrust his fellow-workers. Hypochondria, an evil which he inherited from his unfortunate mother, seized and nearly crazed him. He began to envy Wolke, the first teacher of the Philanthropin, and had a falling out with him and Campe. His distracted mind tortured him with terrific phantoms. He believed all his philanthropic

efforts wrecked, the strain of many years of hard and
honest work a hopeless failure. His loving heart,
which always labored for the happiness of others, felt
bitter remorse. Campe, who is perhaps best known as
the writer of "Robinson Crusoe the Younger," which
has been translated into nearly every European language,
left the institution in 1771, to open a Philanthropin of
his own near Hamburg. Basedow became once more the
director of the school.

Retires.—He was now fifty-five years old. Continued
overwork had made him old, feeble, and sickly. He
resigned his post as Director in 1778, but remained an
interested friend of his Philanthropin to the end of his
life.

Conducts Experiments in Teaching Again.—He now
went to Magdeburg every year for several months,
to teach a class of little girls in a private school. He
did this because of the delight he had in teaching
children, and to try experiments in education. His
whole personality was best adapted for elementary education: he knew the art of making going to school a
pleasure for the little ones; he could make every study
attractive, as he commanded an unlimited amount of
little plans and devices to stimulate and retain attention and an eager desire for knowledge. Physical exercises went hand in hand with mental exertions. Every
lesson appealed to the observant powers of the children,
and invited them to investigate and discover for themselves. Their conception found delightful aids in the

many little stories, references to personal experiences, and pictures which Basedow had ever ready for them. Besides, he always brought a cheerful disposition into the class-room ; so that the little five and six year old children loved and respected the kind old gentleman. They knew, without being told, that he was giving them of his best, always working for their happiness.

Letter Eating.—Basedow had invented a little device to teach his little pupils the rudiments of reading. He had biscuits baked in the form of letters, and let the children eat all letters which they could name. Children are materialistic ever; and the little girls greatly enjoyed these reading lessons. They learned to read fluently in a few weeks. Basedow was pleased, and hoped to see his device adopted by other teachers. Accordingly he published in 1787 the "New Instrument for Learning to Read," describing the scheme at some length, and adding a plan for its introduction.

Whatever has been said and may yet be said of the novel device, it must be admitted that it did away with a great many of the difficulties and the drudgery of the old alphabetic method, and made it palatable, and not only in the true sense of the word at that. What more can be asked of this device? "That freak of Basedow's" was a happy and healthy stimulus. If we had only a few more inventions of this sort! They come from loving hearts, working for the happiness of the dear little learners.

Death.—After the death of his wife (1788) Basedow devoted himself entirely to the education of his son, to prepare him for the university. On the 24th of July, 1790, while at Magdeburg, he was suddenly taken ill. On the 25th, feeling that his end was drawing nigh, he called his son to his bedside, and spoke to him in words of tenderness of the approaching death. At two o'clock in the afternoon the great educational reformer died. His last words were: "I wish my body to be dissected for the benefit of my fellow-men." He was buried in the Holy Spirit Cemetery, at Magdeburg. Over his grave friends and grateful pupils have erected a simple monument.

Close of the Institution.—The Philanthropin at Dessau closed in 1793. Its teachers were scattered about in all parts of Germany, and each applied Basedow's ideas according to his own plan. Many of them set up new schools. The one founded by Salzmann was the world-renowned Philanthropin at Schnepfenthal which still exists. Schlosser, the author of the "History of the Eighteenth Century," who, by the way, is not at all an admirer of Basedow, writes: "Basedow's own institution, after a momentary effulgence, again disappeared, not, however, without leaving considerable traces behind and enlightening the succeeding generation. The effects were only mediate, but they were not on that account less considerable and comprehensive. The whole nature of the school system has undergone a thorough change among us in our century, in some places earlier and in some later. The authorities awoke from their long slumber as a new generation took their seats. German institutions were established, in which an education was given calculated to qualify men for the practical business life; the middle classes were trained and taught as their circumstances of life required them to be; and the female sex, whose education had previously been completely neglected, was rescued from their servile condition to which it had been condemned."

Basedow's Ideas on Education.

Some General Principles.—1. "The aim of education shall be to prepare children to a generally useful, patriotic, and happy life." Happiness Basedow would define in the words of John Locke: "*A sound mind in a sound body* is a short but full description of a happy state in the world."

2. Education is the harmonious development and exercise of the child's powers.

3. The aim of culture is "the formation of character."

4. Instruction forms an important and necessary part of the general plan of education. Still it is relatively of least importance. The formation of character is of greater worth. Instruction that does not educate is of no value whatever.

Family School and State.—Parents are naturally the first rightful and most responsible educators. But they must qualify themselves for their duties, and must work in harmony. They should consult with experienced and successful educators on the best means and methods. "It is necessary for a good education that children have much intercourse with children." Parents must co-operate with the school. "Three or four families might well get together for the purpose of facilitating the education of their children, to convene often to decide on good plans and to execute them."

"Parents who have the necessary means and are able to judge private tutors for themselves, may choose such tutors. Otherwise the public schools are better. The two are also easily combined."

Education and instruction should be a state affair. The state may appoint a "council of education and studies," with full administrative powers in everything pertaining to education. This council should be composed of competent educators, and should have jurisdiction over all asylums of the poor, reformatory schools, orphans' homes, common schools, colleges, universities, the teaching profession, libraries, theatres, and other educational factors. The primary and secondary schools, especially, must be under its direct control. It is to give special attention to the condition and character of school-houses. It shall appoint qualified teachers, and will be held responsible to the nation for those to whom they entrust the education of children.

Teachers.—Teaching is a profession which only those should be allowed to enter who are qualified. The teacher must have pursued a course of professional training. His character must be above reproach. He should be fond of children, love his profession, and must have a natural talent of learning easily what he does not know. It is not necessary that he be thoroughly acquainted with all the common branches. It is sufficient if he has some knowledge of that which he is to teach, and is willing to attend to his own improvement while instructing. It is necessary, however, that he know *how to teach.* Besides, he should be healthy, and have a normally shaped body. Well-qualified teachers should be given a certificate of good character and professional capacity by the council of education. After a few years of successful work in the school, room, they should be appointed for life, *without an examination.* If they discharge their duties faithfully, they ought to be rewarded by the state.

Physical Education.—The educator must be above the dictates of fashion: nature should be his guide. It is his duty to look to the preservation of health, and to strengthen and exercise the physical powers of the child. "Children are fond of movement and noise. They hate to sit still for a long time, more even than a continued strain of attention and learning by rote. Only by force can they be trained to such vexatious employments. That is a warning hint of nature, which parents and guardians seldom heed. Through this criminal disobedience they not only destroy the health of the little ones, but weaken also the intellect and their natural desire for knowledge."

"Wrestling and the other parts of gymnastics or exercises of the body should be restored." Manual training, drawing, and painting are necessary parts in a complete education. "Boys need many little things for their amusement, such as wagons, tops, sticks, and other woodwork. How many of them would often assemble, if encouraged, and each one bring for mutual amusement that which he had learned to make himself! I beg any one of our moral authors who understands the nature of manual work better, to change this important proposition into a complete plan. The carpenter, the cartwright, the smith, the weaver, the bookbinder, the apothecary, and the grocer could be persuaded sometimes to instruct the boys."

The Intellect.—"A child whose acutest faculties are his senses, and who has no perception of anything abstract, must first of all be made acquainted with the world as it presents itself to the senses. Let this be shown him in nature, or, where this is impossible, in faithful drawings and models. Thereby can he even in play, learn how the various objects are to be named.

Comenius alone has pointed out the right road in this matter. By all means reduce the wretched exercise of the memory. "This objective teaching must really furnish the mind with new ideas, not fill up the memory with mere words. Schools and teachers make themselves guilty of a pernicious pedantry if they substitute a knowledge of words in place of the knowledge of things."

The Sensibilities.—The motive of all our actions is self-love. "Every desire is a part of this self-love. We have in our soul also a natural love toward men. Their desires are our own desires, and to satisfy them is our own pleasure." Education must develop philanthropy in the child.

The Will.—All education aims chiefly at the development of tho will. "It consists in habituating the child to discern the useful from the harmful, and to do the right and avoid the wrong. The foundation is obedience to conscience and duty. The motives for obedience are love and confidence." Reason, but at the same time also strict obedience, must control the will. The earliest youth is the time of blind obedience. After years there comes the time when it is advisable to change all commands into good advice."

Morality.—"The moral rules, if they are not confirmed through narrations, occupy only the intellect, but not at the same time the imagination. The most powerful teachings of conduct are self-seen examples and narrations."

Principles of Instruction.—1. The primary object of education should never be forgotten.

2. "Instruction as pleasant as its nature permits."

3. "Proceed from the easy to the difficult in 'elementary' order."

4. Facts are worth more than words.

5. "Not much, but downright useful knowledge, which can never be forgotten without proving a great loss to the individual."

Teaching the Branches.—Language lessons must be lessons *in*, not *on*, language. "I am of the opinion that one can become a masterly writer in a language without ever knowing anything of its grammar. Reason and a wealth of knowledge and words teaches us to write *intelligently,* and through the exercise of taste for good authors we learn to write *well*" (that is, have a good style). But "I do not intend to banish grammar from the number of studies: I only want to assign to it the right place,—which is after the end of the exercises in fluency."

In Arithmetic the child must gain an idea of the value of numbers, and learn to compute with them so as to satisfy the demands of practical life in this direction.

In Geography proceed from the near to the remote. "The beginning from the ground-plan of a room, dwelling, city, and well-known region, and then first the progression to a map of a smaller and larger country to the great divisions of the globe, is something of importance."

"In a certain degree every boy must learn the use of those tools of carpenters, joiners, wood-turners, blacksmiths, masons, and gardeners which are often needed in every household. He ought to be able to help himself in case of need."

Hardening of the body and gymnastic exercises must be insisted upon. They strengthen and develop many valuable powers of the child. "Thus only will we educate true men."

"Up to this time they have educated only learned men, noblemen, or tradesmen. *Men, true men,* are of much greater concern to the world."

APPENDIX.

---

5. "Every pupil knows in every occupation and at all hours whom he owes obedience." We insist upon blind or monastic obedience when the child is under twelve years of age. The older pupils may, if the object permits delay, ask for an explanation of an order, and shall have permission to give their own opinions and desires in return.

6. Only the mechanical work of a pupil shall be disciplined by punishment. Mental work shall be fostered by facilitation, gradual progression, example, persuasion, and instruction. No pupil will be forced to be diligent in his studies.

7. A pupil is not required to learn by rote as long as he is not twelve years old. Everything shall be done, however, that will make the acquisition of knowledge pleasurable and successful, as far as each pupil's gifts can be developed.

8. Our time-table, omitting the hours devoted to sleep, comprises 17 hours, and shall be observed as follows:

(1) Eating, drinking, dressing, and amusements of the pupil's own choice, 6 hours.

(2) Arranging the room, dress, tools, books, bills, and letters, 1 hour.

(3) Studying, 5 hours.

(4) Regulated amusements, such as dancing, riding, fencing, music, etc., 3 hours.

9. Systematic manual work, 2 hours.

10. Those who are very ill-tempered shall be treated as though they were ill bodily. They shall endure confinement, solitude, and rest in their room and bed, etc.

12. All pupils shall be drilled in all military movements and positions. These exercises will be conducted by an expert teacher.

16. During the hours of instruction, our pupils are not required to be in their seats, except for writing, drawing, and reading. They shall never be asked to sit still for more than two or three hours each day, before they are fifteen years old. They may stand, walk, and move about as much as possible.

Geography, for instance, shall be taught in the open air. Two large hemispheres may be made of the ground of the earth, their surface showing the different forms of land and water. They must not be entirely round, but curved only a little, so as to enable the pupils to walk and jump around on them.

Altogether, the necessary memory work of history, geography, arithmetic, etc., shall be changed into play, connected with amusement and plenty of movement. This shall be continued until the knowledge thus ac-

quired enables the student, when older, to perfect himself in a more manly way.

But of all the certainly very useful studies in language, science, and dexterity, nothing shall be as important as the *formation of character;* i.e., the development
of the natural, innate germs to philanthropy, virtue,
and innocent contentment.

Allen's Mind Studies for Young Teach-

ERS. By JEROME ALLEN, Ph.D., Associate Editor of the
SCHOOL JOURNAL, Prof. of Pedagogy, Univ. of City of
N. Y. 16mo, large, clear type, 128 pp. Cloth, 50 cents; *to
teachers*, 40 cents; by mail, 5 cents extra.

There are many teachers who know little about psychology, and who desire to be better informed concerning its principles, especially its relation to the work of teaching. For the aid of such, this book has been prepared. But it is not a psychology—only an introduction to it, aiming to give some fundamental principles, together with something concerning the philosophy of education. Its method is subjective rather than objective, leading the student to watch mental processes, and draw his own conclusions. It is written in language easy to be comprehended, and has many practical illustrations. It will aid the teacher in his daily work in dealing with mental facts and states.

JEROME ALLEN, Ph.D..Associate Editor of the *Journal* and *Institute.*

To most teachers psychology seems to be dry. This book shows how it may become the most interesting of all studies. It also shows how to begin the knowledge of self. "We cannot know in others what we do not first know in ourselves." This is the key-note of this book. Students of elementary psychology will appreciate this feature of "Mind Studies."

ITS CONTENTS.

Allen's Temperament in Education.

With directions concerning How TO BECOME A SUCCESSFUL
TEACHER. By JEROME ALLEN, Ph.D., Author of "Mind
Studies for Young Teachers," etc.   Cloth, 16mo.   Price, 50
cents, *to teachers*, 40 cents; by mail, 5 cents extra.

There is no book in the English language accessible to
students on this important subject, yet it is a topic of so much
importance to all who wish to become better acquainted with
themselves that its suggestions will find a warm welcome
everywhere, especially by teachers. The value of the book will
be readily seen by noticing the subjects discussed.

CONTENTS:—How we can know Mind—Native Characteristics of
Children—How to Study Ourselves—The Sanguine Temperament—The
Bilious Temperament—The Lymphatic Temperament—The Nervous
Temperament—Physical Characteristics of each Temperament: Tabula-
ted—The *best* Temperament—How to Conduct Self Study—Many Per-
sonal Questions for Students of Themselves—How to Improve—Specific
Directions—How to Study Children—How Children are Alike, How
Different—Facts in Child Growth: Tabulated and Explained—How to
Promote Healthy Child Growth. Full directions concerning how to
treat temperamental differences. How to effect change in temperament.

Under "How TO BECOME A SUCCESSFUL TEACHER," the
following topics are discussed: "What books and papers to
read."—"What schools to visit."—"What associates to select."
—"What subjects to study."—"How to find helpful critics."—
"How to get the greatest good from institutes."—"Shall I
attend a Normal school?"   "How to get a good and perman-
ent position?"   "How to get good pay?"   "How to grow a
better teacher year after year."   "Professional honesty and
dishonesty."—"The best and most enduring reward."

Blaikie's Self Culture,

By JOHN STUART BLAIKIE.   16mo, 64 pp., limp cloth.   Price, 25
cents; *to teachers*, 20 cents; by mail, 3 cents extra.

Three invaluable practical essays on the Culture of the Intellect, on Physical Culture, on Moral Culture. In its 64 pages this
little volume contains a vast amount of excellent advice. It will
help hundreds of young teachers to make a right start, or set
them right if they are on the wrong track. Although published
expressly for teachers, it will prove profitable reading for all, no
matter what their calling, who wish to improve—and who does
not? As a part of a course of reading, some such book is invaluable, and should be read over and over again. Mr. Blaikie's book,
in its present form, is so neat yet cheap, that it ought to be read
by every young teacher in the country, and to be on every reading-circle list. It is to be a prominent book on the new professional course of reading for teachers.

Nicely printed. with side-heads and bound in limp ᵃlᵒᵗʰ.

Analytical Questions Series.

No. 1. GEOGRAPHY. 126 pp.
No. 2. HISTORY OF THE UNITED STATES. 108 pp.
No. 3. GRAMMAR. 104 pp.

Price 50c. each; to teachers, 40c; by mail, 5c. extra. The three for $1.20, postpaid. *Each complete with answers.*

This new series of question-books is prepared for teachers by a teacher of high standing and wide experience. Every possible advantage in arrangement of other books was adopted in these, and several very important new ones added. The most important is the

GRADING OF QUESTIONS

into three grades, thus enabling the teacher to advance in her knowledge by easy steps.

THE ANALYTICAL FEATURE

is also prominent—the questions being divided into paragraphs of ten each, under its appropriate heading.

TYPOGRAPHY AND BINDING.

Type is clear and large, and printing and paper the very best, while the binding is in our usual tasteful and durable style, in cloth.

The books are well adapted for use in schools where a compact general review of the whole subject is desired. The answers have been written out in full and complete statements, and have been separated from the body of the questions with a view of enforcing and facilitating the most profitable study of the subject. The author has asked every conceivable question that would be likely to come up in the most rigid examination. There are other question-books published, but even the largest is not so complete on a single branch as these.

Bear in mind that these question-books are absolutely without a rival

FOR PREPARING FOR EXAMINATION,
FOR REVIEWING PUPILS IN SCHOOL,
FOR USE AS REFERENCE BOOKS.

The slightest examination of this series will decide you in its favor over any other similar books.

Augsburg's Easy Things to Draw.

By D. R. AUGSBURG, Supt. Drawing at Salt Lake City, Utah.
Quarto, durable and elegant cardboard cover, 80 pp., with
31 pages of plates, containing over 200 different figures.
Price, 30 cents; *to teachers*, 24 cents; by mail, 4 cents extra.

This book is not designed to present a system of drawing. It
is a collection of drawings made in the simplest possible way, and
so constructed that any one may reproduce them. Its design is
to furnish a hand-book containing drawings as would be needed
for the school-room for object lessons, drawing lessons, busy
work. This collection may be used in connection with any system of drawing, as it contains examples suitable for practice. It
may also be used alone, as a means of learning the art of drawing. As will be seen from the above the idea of this book is new
and novel. Those who have seen it are delighted with it as it so
exactly fills a want. An index enables the teacher to refer instantly to a simple drawing of a cat, dog, lion, coffee-berry, etc.
Our list of Blackboard Stencils is in the same line.

Augsburg's Easy Drawings for the Geo-

GRAPHY CLASS. By D. R. AUGSBURG, B. P., author of "Easy
Things to Draw." Contains 40 large plates, each containing
from 4 to 60 separate drawings. 96 pp., quarto cardboard
cover. Price 50 cents; *to teachers*, 40 cents; by mail 5 cents
extra.

In this volume is the same excellent work that was noted in Mr.
Augsburg's "Easy Things to Draw." He does not here seek to
present a system of drawing, but to give a collection of drawings
made in the simplest possible way, and so constructed that any
one may reproduce them. Leading educators believe that drawing has not occupied the position in the school course hereto-
fore that it ought to have occupied: that it is the most effectual
means of presenting facts, especially in the sciences. The author
has used it in this book to illustrate geography, giving drawings of plants, animals, and natural features, and calling attention to steps in drawing. The idea is a novel one, and it is
believed that the practical manner in which the subject is treated
will make the book a popular one in the school-room. Each
plate is placed opposite a lesson that may be used in connection.
An index brings the plates instantly to the eye.

Calkins' Ear and Voice Training by

MEANS OF ELEMENTARY SOUNDS OF LANGUAGE. By N. A.
CALKINS, Assistant Superintendent N. Y. City Schools;
author of "Primary Object Lessons," "Manual of Object
Teaching," "Phonic Charts," etc. Cloth. 16mo, about 100
pp. Price, 50 cents; *to teachers*, 40 cents; by mail, 5 cents extra.

An idea of the character of this work may be had by the following extracts from its *Preface:*

"The common existence of abnormal sense perception among school
children is a serious obstacle in teaching. This condition is most
obvious in the defective perceptions
of sounds and forms. It may be
seen in the faulty articulations in
speaking and reading; in the inability to distinguish musical sounds
readily; also in the common mistakes made in hearing what is
said. . . .

"Careful observation and long
experience lead to the conclusion
that the most common defects in
sound perceptions exist because of
lack of proper training in childhood
to develop this power of the mind
into activity through the sense of
hearing. It becomes, therefore, a
matter of great importance in education, that in the training of children due attention shall be given to
the development of ready and accurate perceptions of sounds.

"How to give this training so as
to secure the desired results is a
subject that deserves the careful
attention of parents and teachers.

SUPT. N. A. CALKINS.

Much depends upon the manner of
presenting the sounds of our language to pupils, whether or not the
results shall be the development in sound-perceptions that will *train
the ear and voice* to habits of distinctness and accuracy in speaking and
reading.

"The methods of teaching given in this book are the results of an
extended experience under such varied conditions as may be found
with pupils representing all nationalities, both of native and foreign
born children. The plans described will enable teachers to lead their
pupils to acquire ready and distinct perceptions through sense training, and cause them to know the sounds of our language in a manner
that will give practical aid in learning both the spoken and the written
language. The simplicity and usefulness of the lessons need only to be
known to be appreciated and used."

Dewey's How to Teach Manners in the

SCHOOL-ROOM. By Mrs. JULIA M. DEWEY, Principal of the Normal School at Lowell, Mass., formerly Supt. of Schools at Hoosick Falls, N. Y. Cloth, 16mo, 104 pp. Price, 50 cents; *to teachers*, 40 cents; by mail, 5 cents extra.

Many teachers consider the manners of a pupil of little importance so long as he is industrious. But the boys and girls are to be fathers and mothers; some of the boys will stand in places of importance as professional men, and they will carry the mark of ill-breeding all their lives. Manners can be taught in the school-room: they render the school-room more attractive; they banish tendencies to misbehavior. In this volume Mrs. Dewey has shown how manners can be taught. The method is to present some fact of deportment, and then lead the children to discuss its bearings; thus they learn why good manners are to be learned and practised. The printing and binding are exceedingly neat and attractive."

OUTLINE OF CONTENTS.

Introduction.
General Directions.
Special Directions to Teachers.

LESSONS ON MANNERS FOR YOUNGEST PUPILS.

Lessons on Manners — Second Two Years.
Manners in School—First Two Years.
" " Second "
Manners at Home—First "
" " Second "
Manners in Public—First "
" " Second "

Table Manners—First Two Years.
" " Second "

LESSONS ON MANNERS FOR ADVANCED PUPILS.
Manners in School.
Personal Habits.
Manners in Public.
Table Manners.
Manners in Society.
Miscellaneous Items.
Practical Training in Manners.
Suggestive Stories, Fables, Anecdotes, and Poems.
Memory Gems.

Central School Journal.—"It furnishes illustrative lessons."

Texas School Journal.—"They (the pupils) will carry the mark of ill-breeding all their lives (unless taught otherwise)."

Pacific Ed. Journal.—"Principles are enforced by anecdote and conversation."

Teacher's Exponent.—"We believe such a book will be very welcome."

National Educator.—"Common-sense suggestions."

Ohio Ed. Monthly.—"Teachers would do well to get it."

Nebraska Teacher.—"Many teachers consider manners of little importance, but some of the boys will stand in places of importance."

School Educator.—"The spirit of the author is commendable."

School Herald.—"These lessons are full of suggestions."

Va. School Journal.—"Lessons furnished in a delightful style."

Miss. Teacher.—"The best presentation we have seen."

Ed. Courant.—"It is simple, straightforward, and plain."

Iowa Normal Monthly.—"Practical and well-arranged lessons on manners."

Progressive Educator.—"Will prove to be most helpful to the teacher who desires her pupils to be well-mannered."

Froebel. Autobiography of

MATERIALS TO AID A COMPREHENSION OF THE WORKS OF THE FOUNDER OF THE KINDERGARTEN. 16mo, large, clear type, 128 pp. Cloth, 16mo, 50 cents; *to teachers*, 40 cents; by mail, 5 cents extra.

This little volume will be welcomed by all who want to get a good idea of Froebel and the kindergarten.

This volume contains besides the autobiography—

1. Important dates connected with the kindergarten.

2. Froebel and the kindergarten system of education by Joseph Payne.

3. Froebel and his educational work.

4. Frœbel's educational views (a summary).

In this volume the student of education will find materials for constructing, in an intelligent manner, an estimate and comprehension of the kindergarten. The life of Froebel, mainly by his own hand, is very helpful. In this we see the working of his mind when a youth; he lets us see how he felt at being misunderstood, at being called a bad

FREIDRICH FROEBEL.

boy, and his pleasure when face to face with Nature. Gradually we see there was crystallizing in him a comprehension of the means that would bring harmony and peace to the minds of young people.

The analysis of the views of Froebel will be of great aid. We see that there was a deep philosophy in this plain German man; he was studying out a plan by which the usually wasted years of young children could be made productive. The volume will be of great value not only to every kindergartner, but to all who wish to understand the philosophy of mental development.

La. Journal of Education.—"An excellent little work."

W. Va. School Journal.—"Will be of great value."

Educational Courant, Ky.—"Ought to have a very extensive circulation among the teachers of the country."

Educational Record, Can.—"Ought to be in the hands of every professional teacher."

Western School Journal.—"Teachers will find in this a clear account of Froebel's life."

School Education.—"Froebel tells his own story better than any commentator."

Michigan Moderator.—"Will be of great value to all who wish to understand the philosophy of mental development."

Hughes' Mistakes in Teaching.

By JAMES J. HUGHES, Inspector of Schools, Toronto, **Canada.**
Cloth, 16mo, 115 pp. Price, 50 cents; *to teachers,* 40 cents;
by mail, 5 cents extra.

Thousands of copies of the old edition have been sold. The new edition is worth double the old; the material has been increased, restated, and greatly improved. Two new and important Chapters have been added on "Mistakes in Aims," and "Mistakes in Moral Training." Mr. Hughes says in his preface: "In issuing a revised edition of this book, it seems fitting to acknowledge gratefully the hearty appreciation that has been accorded it by American teachers. Realizing as I do that its very large sale indicates that it has been of service to many of my fellow-teachers, I have recognized the duty of enlarging and revising it so as to make it still more helpful in preventing the common mistakes in teaching and training."

JAMES L. HUGHES, Inspector of
Schools, Toronto, Canada.

This is one of the six books recommended by the N. Y. State Department to teachers preparing for examination for State certificates.

CAUTION.

Our new AUTHORIZED COPYRIGHT EDITION, *entirely rewritten by the author, is the only one to buy. It is beautifully printed and handsomely bound. Get no other.*

CONTENTS OF OUR NEW EDITION.

CHAP. I. 7 Mistakes in Aim.
CHAP. II. 21 Mistakes in School Management.
CHAP. III. 24 Mistakes in Discipline.
CHAP. IV. 27 Mistakes in Method.
CHAP. V. 13 Mistakes in Moral Training.

☞ *Chaps. I. and V. are entirely new.*

Johnson's Education by Doing.

Education by Doing: A Book of Educative Occupations for Children in School. By ANNA JOHNSON, teacher to the Children's Aid Schools of New York City. With a prefatory note by Edward R. Shaw, of the High School of Yonkers, N. Y. Handsome red cloth, gilt stamp. Price, 75 cents; *to teachers*, 60 cents; by mail, 5 cents extra.

Thousands of teachers are asking the question: "How can I keep my pupils profitably occupied?" This book answers the question. Theories are omitted. Every line is full of instruction.

1. Arithmetic is taught with blocks, beads, toy-money, etc.
2. The tables are taught by clock dials, weights, etc.
3. Form is taught by blocks.
4. Lines with sticks.
5. Language with pictures.
6. Occupations are given.
7. Everything is plain and practical.

EXTRACT FROM PREFATORY NOTE.

"In observing the results achieved by the Kindergarten, educators have felt that Froebel's great discovery of education by occupations must have something for the public schools—that a further application of the 'putting of experience and action in the place of books and abstract thinking, could be made beyond the fifth or sixth year of the child's life. This book is an outgrowth of this idea, conceived in the spirit of the 'New Education.'

"It will be widely welcomed, we believe, as it gives concrete methods of work—the very aids primary teachers are in search of. There has been a wide discussion of the subject of education, and there exists no little confusion in the mind of many a teacher as to how he should improve upon methods that have been condemned."

Supt. J. W. Skinner, Children's Aid Schools, says:—"It is highly appreciated by our teachers. It supplies a want felt by all."

Toledo Blade.—"The need of this book has been felt by teachers."

School Education.—"Contains a great many fruitful suggestions."

Christian Advance.—"The method is certainly philosophical."

Va. Ed. Journal.—"The book is an outgrowth of Froebel's idea."

Philadelphia Teacher.—"The book is full of practical information."

Iowa Teacher.—"Kellogg's books are all good, but this is the best for teachers."

The Educationist.—"We regard it as very valuable."

School Bulletin.—"We think well of this book."

Chicago Intelligence.—"Will be found a very serviceable book."

Love's Industrial Education.

Industrial Education ; a guide to Manual Training. By
SAMUEL G. LOVE, principal of the Jamestown, (N. Y.)
public schools. Cloth, 12mo, 330 pp. with 40 full-page
plates containing nearly 400 figures. Price, $1.50; *to
teachers*, $1.20 ; by mail, 12 cents extra.

1. *Industrial Education not understood.* Probably the only
man who has wrought out the problem in a practical way is
Samuel G. Love, the superintendent of the Jamestown (N.
Y.) schools. Mr. Love has now about 2,400 children in the primary, advanced, and high schools under his charge ; he is assisted by fifty teachers, so that an admirable opportunity was offered. In 1874 (about fourteen years ago) Mr. Love began his experiment ; gradually he introduced one occupation, and then another, until at last nearly all the pupils are following some form of educating work.

2. *Why it is demanded.* The reasons for introducing it are clearly stated by Mr. Love. It was done because the education of the books left the pupils unfitted to meet the practical problems the world asks them to solve. The world does not have a field ready for the student in book-lore. The statements of Mr. Love should be carefully read.

3. *It is an educational book.* Any one can give some formal work to girls and boys. What has been needed has been some one who could find out what is suited to the little child who is in the " First Reader," to the one who is in the "Second Reader," and so on. It must be remembered the effort is not to make carpenters, and type-setters, and dressmakers of boys and girls, but to *educate them by these occupations better than without them.*

Parker's Talks on Teaching.

Notes of "Talks on Teaching" given by COL. FRANCIS W.
PARKER (formerly Superintendent of schools of Quincy,
Mass.), before the Martha's Vineyard Institute, Summer
of 1882. Reported by LELIA E. PATRIDGE. Square 16mo,
5x6 1-2 inches, 192 pp., *laid* paper, English cloth. Price,
$1.25 ; *to teachers,* $1.00 ; by mail, 9 cents extra.

The methods of teaching employed in the schools of Quincy,
Mass., were seen to be the methods of nature. As they were
copied and explained, they awoke a great desire on the part
of those who could not visit the schools to know the underlying principles. In other words, Colonel Parker was asked to
explain *why* he had his teachers teach thus. In the summer
of 1882, in response to requests, Colonel Parker gave a course
of lectures before the Martha's Vineyard Institute, and these
were reported by Miss Patridge, and published in this book.

The book became famous ;
more copies were sold of it in
the same time than of any
other educational book whatever. The daily papers, which
usually pass by such books
with a mere mention, devoted
columns to reviews of it.

The following points will
show why the teacher will
want this book.

1. It explains the "New
Methods." There is a wide
gulf between the new and the
old education. Even school
boards understand this.

2. It gives the underlying
principles of education. For it
must be remembered that Col. Parker is not expounding *his*
methods, but the methods of nature.

3. It gives the ideas of man who is evidently an "educational genius," a man born to understand and expound education. We have few such ; they are worth everything to the
human race.

4. It gives a biography of Col. Parker. This will help the
teacher of education to comprehend the man and his motives.

5. It has been adopted by nearly every State Reading Circle

The Practical Teacher.

Writings of FRANCIS W. PARKER, Principal of Cook Co. Normal School, Ill., and other educators, among which is Joseph Payne's Visit to German Schools, etc. 188 large 8vo pages, 7¼ x 10¼ inches. Cloth. Price, $1.50; *to teachers*, $1.20; by mail, 14 cents extra. New edition in paper cover. Price, 75 cents; *to teachers*, 60 cents; by mail, 8 cents extra.

These articles contain many things that the readers of the "Talks on Teaching" desired light upon. The space occupied enabled Col. Parker to state himself at the length needed for clearness. There is really here, from his pen (taking out the writings of others) a volume of 330 pages, each page about the size of those in "Talks on Teaching."

1. The writings in this volume are mainly those of Col. F. W. Parker, Principal of the Cook County Normal School.

2. Like the "Talks on Teaching" so famous, they deal with the principles and practice of teaching.

3. Those who own the "Talks" will want the further ideas from Col. Parker.

4. There are many things in this volume written in reply to inquiries suggested in "Talks."

5. There is here really 750 pages of the size of those in "Talks." "Talks" sells for $1.00. This for $1.20 and 14 cents for postage.

6. Minute suggestions are made pertaining to Reading, Questions, Geography, Numbers, History, Psychology, Pedagogics, Clay Modeling, Form, Color, etc.

7. Joseph Payne's visit to the German schools is given in full; everything from his pen is valuable.

8. The whole book has the breeze that is blowing from the New Education ideas; it is filled with Col. Parker's spirit.

PARTIAL LIST OF CONTENTS.

Quick's Educational Reformers.

By Rev. ROBERT HERBERT QUICK, M. A., of Trinity College, Cambridge, England. Bound in plain, but elegant cloth binding. 16mo, about 350 pp. $1.00; *to teachers*, 80 cts.; by mail, 10 cts. extra.

New edition with topical headings, chronological table and other aids for systematic study in normal schools and reading-circles.

No book in the history of education has been so justly popular as this. Mr. Quick has the remarkable faculty of grasping the salient points of the work of the great educators, and restating their ideas in clear and vigorous language.

This book supplies information that is contained in no other single volume, touching the progress of education in its earliest stages after the revival of learning. It is the work of a practical teacher, who supplements his sketches of famous educationists with some well-considered observations, that deserve the attention of all who are interested in that subject. Beginning with Roger Ascham, it gives an account of the lives and schemes of most of the great thinkers and workers in the educational field, down to Herbert Spencer, with the addition of a valuable appendix of thoughts and suggestions on teaching. The list includes the names of Montaigne, Ratich, Milton, Comenius, Locke, Rousseau, Basedow, Pestalozzi, and Jacotot. In the lives and thoughts of these eminent men is presented the whole philosophy of education, as developed in the progress of modern times.

This book has been adopted by nearly every state reading-circle in the country, and purchased by thousands of teachers, and is used in many normal schools.

Contents: 1. Schools of the Jesuits; 2. Ascham, Montaigne, Ratich, Milton: 3. Comenius; 4. Locke: 5. Rousseau's Emile; 6. Basedow and the Philanthropin; 7. Pestalozzi; 8. Jacotot; 9. Herbert Spencer; 10. Thoughts and Suggestions about Teaching Children; 11. Some Remarks about Moral and Religious Education; 12. Appendix.

OUR NEW EDITION.

Be sure to get E. L. Kellogg's edition. There are other editions in the market that are not only higher in price, but very inferior in binding and typography and without the paragraph headings that are so useful. Our edition is complete with all these improvements, is beautifully printed and exquisitely bound in cloth, and the retail price is only $1.00, with discounts to teachers and reading-circles.

Reinhart's Outline History of Education.

With chronological Tables, Suggestions, and Test Questions. By J. A. REINHART, Ph. D. Teachers' Professional Library. 77 pp., limp cloth, 25 cents; *to teachers*, 20 cents; by mail 2 cents extra.

This is one of the little books intended to be studied in connection with THE TEACHERS' PROFESSION. The publishers, by means of these publications bring to the very doors of those teachers who lack the opportunity to attend a normal school a chance to improve in the art of teaching. " Outlines of History of Education " is what its name implies, a brief but comprehensive presentation of the main facts in educational progress. The chapters are: Introduction; Education among the Greeks; Education among the Romans; Education in the Middle Ages; the Dawn of the New Era; Education and the Reformation; Education in the Seventeenth Century; Education in the Eighteenth Century; Education in the Nineteenth Century. A thorough study of this book will be a good foundation for a more detailed study of the subject. The book is well printed from clear, large type, with topic heads and questions, and is durably bound in limp cloth.

Reinhart's Outline Principles of Education

By J. A. REINHART., Ph. D. Teachers' Professional Library. 68 pp., limp cloth, 25 cents.

To give an outline of a great subject, including nothing trivial and leaving out nothing important, is a great art. This difficult task has been successfully performed by the author of this small volume, who is an educator of long experience, and a thorough student of the science of education. The first two chapters give a general view of the subject, and the other chapters treat of the intuitive, imaginative, and logical stages of education, and the principles of moral education. This is one of the volumes intended to be studied in connection with the monthly paper, THE TEACHERS' PROFESSION. Type, printing, binding are neat and durable, and like the History by same author.

REINHART'S CIVICS IN EDUCATION,

is another little book of same price and number of pages. Ready Nov. 1891.

Seeley's Grube's Method of Teaching

ARITHMETIC. Explained and illustrated. Also the improvements on the method made by the followers of Grubé in Germany. By LEVI SEELEY, Ph.D. Cloth, 176 pp. Price, $1.00; *to teachers* 80 cents; by mail, 7 cents extra.

1. IT IS A PHILOSOPHICAL WORK.—This book has a sound philosophical basis. The child does not (as most teachers seem to think) learn addition, then subtraction, then multiplication, then division; he learns these processes together. Grubé saw this, and founded his system on this fact.

2. IT FOLLOWS NATURE'S PLAN.—Grubé proceeds to develop (so to speak) the method by which the child actually becomes (if he ever does) acquainted with 1, 2, 3, 4, 5, etc. This is not done, as some suppose, by writing them on a slate. Nature has her method; she begins with THINGS; after handling two things in certain ways, the idea of *two* is obtained, and so of other numbers. *The chief value of this book then consists in showing what may be termed the way nature teaches the child number.*

DR. LEVI SEELEY.

3. IT IS VALUABLE TO PRIMARY TEACHERS.—It begins and shows how the child can be taught 1, then 2, then 3, &c. Hence it is a work especially valuable for the primary teacher. It gives much space to showing how the numbers up to 10 are taught; for if this be correctly done, the pupil will almost teach himself the rest.

4. IT CAN BE USED IN ADVANCED GRADES.—It discusses methods of teaching fractions, percentage, etc., so that it is a work valuable for all classes of teachers.

5 IT GUIDES THE TEACHER'S WORK.—It shows, for example, what the teacher can appropriately do the first year, what the second, the third, and the fourth. More than this, it suggests work for the teacher she would otherwise omit.

Taking it altogether, it is the best work on teaching *number* ever published. It is very handsomely printed and bound.

Prof. E. A. Sheldon, Ph.D., President Oswego Normal School, N. Y. " It is an admirable presentation of the method. It seems to me the best that has been given us. The number of practical examples and the clearness with which every point is presented are admirable features."

Prof. Eugene Bouton, Principal Normal School, New Paltz, N. Y. " It throws new and needed light on the subject of teaching arithmetic. Every teacher owes the author a double gratitude; all will welcome so complete and intelligible an exposition of the system."

Prof. Thomas M. Balliet, Superintendent of Schools, Springfield, Mass. " It is the best exposition of the Grube Method as now defined by his disciples than exists in English or in German. I know of no one who is more competent to interpret this now famous method than Dr. Seeley."

Wm. C. Roberts, D.D., LL.D., Pres. Lake Forest University, Ill. " It is to be hoped that this philosophical and masterly method of teaching numbers will be introduced and thoroughly tested in the schools of America. No teacher who wishes to keep abreast of the march of progress in the direction of education can afford to be without it."

Supt. L. B. Klemm, Cincinnati, Ohio. " You have done the American school and the vast army of primary teachers in this country a valuable service by offering to the public " Grube's Method " in English garb."

Principal W. E. Gordon, Patchogue, L. I. " Dr. Seeley has presented the Grube Method in a plain and complete manner. The book is full of excellent suggestions for primary schools whether they adopt the Grube Method or not."

Prin. J. E. Young, New Rochelle, N. Y. " If this method were taught we should obtain far better results than we now have. I have prided myself on the work done in my primary classes, but I can see how it can be greatly improved."

Prof. Francis W. Kelly, Lake Forest University, Ill. " This little volume may be accepted as the best pedagogic hand-book of the subject accessible to the teacher. When one sees the time wasted here in teaching arithmetic (compared with Germany) he sees the need of this book."

The Journal of Education, (Boston,) says : The chief value of the book consists in showing the way nature teaches the child numbers."

Seeley's Grube Idea in Teaching Primary

Arithmetic. Elements of the Grubé Method, containing the latest improvements made by Grubé's followers in Germany. Revised, explained, and illustrated for the use of the teachers of America. 12mo, 64 pp., limp cloth cover. Price, 30 cents; *to teachers,* 24 cents; by mail, 3 cents extra.

Very many teachers have called for the primary work only of Mr. Seeley's well-known larger book (which we may say gains year by year in popularity), so he has prepared this little volume. It is printed in large type, with illustrations, and should meet with a large sale among the primary teachers because it expounds the scientific way of teaching the first steps of arithmetic.

Shaw and Donnell's School Devices.

"SCHOOL DEVICES." A book of ways and suggestions for teachers. By EDWARD R. SHAW and WEBB DONNELL, of the High School at Yonkers, N. Y. Illustrated. Dark-blue cloth binding, gold, 16mo, 289 pp. Price, $1.25; *to teachers*, $1.00; by mail, 9 cents extra.

This valuable book has just been greatly improved by the addition of nearly 75 pages of entirely new material.

☞A BOOK OF "WAYS" FOR TEACHERS.☜

Teaching is an art; there are "ways to do it." This book is made to point out "ways," and to help by suggestions.

1. It gives "ways" for teaching Language, Grammar, Reading, Spelling, Geography, etc. These are in many cases novel; they are designed to help attract the attention of the pupil.

2. The "ways" given are not the questionable "ways" so often seen practised in school-rooms, but are in accord with the spirit of modern educational ideas.

3. This book will afford practical assistance to teachers who wish to keep their work from degenerating into mere routine. It gives them, in convenient form for constant use at the desk, a multitude of new ways in which to present old truths. The great enemy of the teacher is want of interest. Their methods do not attract attention. There is no teaching unless there is *attention*. The teacher is too apt to think there is but one "way" of teaching spelling; he thus falls into a rut. Now there are many "ways" of teaching spelling, and some "ways" are better than others. Variety must exist in the school-room; the authors of this volume deserve the thanks of the teachers for pointing out methods of obtaining variety without sacrificing the great end sought—scholarship. New "ways" induce greater effort, and renewal of activity.

4. The book gives the result of large actual experience in the school-room, and will meet the needs of thousands of teachers, by placing at their command that for which visits to other schools are made, institutes and associations attended, viz., new ideas and fresh and forceful ways of teaching. The devices given under Drawing and Physiology are of an eminently practical nature, and cannot fail to invest these subjects with new interest. The attempt has been made to present only devices of a practical character.

5. The book suggests "ways" to make teaching *effective;* it is not simply a book of new "ways," but of "ways" that will produce good results.

Tate's Philosophy of Education.

The Philosophy of Education. By T. TATE. Revised and Annotated by E. E. SHEIB, Ph.D., Principal of the Louisiana State Normal School. Unique cloth binding, laid paper, 331 pp. Price, $1.50; *to teachers*, $1.20; by mail, 7 cents extra.

There are few books that deal with the Science of Education. This volume is the work of a man who said there were great principles at the bottom of the work of the despised schoolmaster. It has set many a teacher to thinking, and in its new form will set many more.

Our edition will be found far superior to any other in every respect. The annotations of Mr. Sheib are invaluable. The more important part of the book are emphasized by leading the type. The type is clear, the size convenient, and printing, paper, and binding are most excellent.

Mr. Philbrick so long superintendent of the Boston schools hold this work in high esteem.

Col. F. W. Parker strongly recommends it.

Jos. MacAlister, Supt. Public Schools, Philadelphia, says :—"It is one of the first books which a teacher deserves of understanding the scientific principles on which his work rests should study."

Graded Examination Questions.

For N. Y. State, from Sept., 1887, to Sept., 1889, *with answers complete.* First, Second, and Third Grades. Cloth, 12mo, 219 pp. Price, $1.00; *to teachers*, 80 cents; by mail, 8 cents extra.

This volume contains the Uniform Graded Examination Questions, issued to the School Commissioners of the State by the Dept. of Public Instruction, commencing Sept., 1887, and ending Aug. 13 and 14, 1889. The answers are also given. These questions have been adopted by all the school commissioners of the State; the test in each county thus becomes uniform. These questions are being used very largely in many other States, that pattern after New York, and will therefore be of far more than local interest. Indeed, teachers and school officers in all States are using these questions as a basis for their own examinations. Our edition is the best in arrangement, print, binding, and has an excellent contents and index.

This book may be used to the best advantage by the teacher who desires to advance in the profession, because the questions are carefully graded. After the lowest grade of questions have been successfully answered, the next higher grade is studies. In our edition the answers are entirely separate from the questions in the back of the book.

Song Treasures.

THE PRICE HAS BEEN
GREATLY REDUCED.

Compiled by AMOS M. KELLOGG, editor of the SCHOOL JOUR-
NAL. Beautiful and durable postal-card manilla cover,
printed in two colors, 64 pp. Price, 15 cents each; *to teachers,*
12 cents; by mail, 2 cents extra. 30th thousand. *Write for
our special terms to schools for quantities. Special terms for use
at Teachers' Institutes.*

This is a most valuable collection of mu-
sic for all
schools and in-
stitutes.

1. Most of the pieces have
been selected
by the teachers
as favorites in
the schools.
They are the
ones the pupils
love to sing.
It contains
nearly 100
pieces.

2. All the pieces "have a ring to them;" they are easily
learned, and will not be forgotten.

3. The themes and words are appropriate for young people.
In these respects the work will be found to possess unusual merit.
Nature, the Flowers, the Seasons, the Home, our Duties, our
Creator, are entuned with beautiful music.

4. Great ideas may find an entrance into the mind through
music. Aspirations for the good, the beautiful, and the true are
presented here in a musical form.

5. Many of the words have been written especially for the
book. One piece, "The Voice Within Us," p. 57, is worth the
price of the book.

6. The titles here given show the teacher what we mean:

**Ask the Children, Beauty Everywhere, Be in Time, Cheerfulness,
Christmas Bells, Days of Summer Glory, The Dearest Spot, Evening Song,
Gentle Words, Going to School, Hold up the Right Hand, I Love the Merry,
Merry Sunshine, Kind Deeds, Over in the Meadows, Our Happy School,
Scatter the Germs of the Beautiful, Time to Walk, The Jolly Workers, The
Teacher's Life, Tribute to Whittier, etc., etc.**